Presented to

_____

On the Occasion of

_____

From

_____

Date

_____

©MCMXCIX by Barbour Publishing, Inc.

ISBN 1-893065-62-6

All Scripture quotations are taken from the King James Version of the Bible.

Published by Barbour Publishing, Inc., P. O. Box 719, Uhrichsville, Ohio 44683
http://www.barbourbooks.com

Member of the
Evangelical Christian
Publishers Association

Printed in the United States of America.

For God So Loved
The World That He Gave His
Only Begotten Son.

FAMILY
CHRISTIAN
PRESS

In Him eternal might and power
To human weakness hath inclined;
And this poor Child brings riches dower
Of gifts and graces to mankind.

FROM "CHRISTIANS, SING OUT WITH EXULTATION,"
BY BENEDICT PICTET (TRANSLATED BY HENRY L. JENNER)

Introduction

Gifts are an expression of love. Often they come in shiny paper and fancy ribbons. Sometimes they have different wrappings.

Some two thousand years ago, the greatest Gift-Giver of all, God the Father, gave the greatest Gift of all, God the Son. The Father wrapped His Gift in the flesh and blood package of humanity, and Jesus Christ was born in a stable in Bethlehem. And the world would never be the same again.

This little book, through Scripture verses and the lyrics of classic carols and hymns, celebrates the Gift. It's a joyous reminder that says, *For God So Loved The World That He Gave His Only Begotten Son.*

Bring your gifts to Mary's Son
(Ring the bells of Christmas).
God's own Gift to everyone;
Blessed Child of Christmas.

FROM "LITTLE CHILDREN, RISE AND SING,"
BY C. E. MACNIVEN

The Gift

Quietly, with little fanfare, God sent His Son to Earth. His humble beginnings gave few indications of the awesome impact His life—and death—would have on the world. Jesus Christ was truly God's greatest Gift of all!

How silently, how silently,
the wondrous Gift is given;
So God imparts to human hearts
the blessings of His heaven.
No ear may hear His coming,
but in this world of sin,
Where meek souls will receive Him still,
the dear Christ enters in.

FROM "O LITTLE TOWN OF BETHLEHEM,"
BY PHILLIPS BROOKS

For unto you is born this day in the city of David a Saviour, which is Christ the Lord.   LUKE 2:11

For God so loved the world, that he gave his only begotten Son, that whosoever believeth in him should not perish, but have everlasting life.   JOHN 3:16

But we see Jesus, who was made a little lower than the angels for the suffering of death, crowned with glory and honour; that he by the grace of God should taste death for every man.

HEBREWS 2:9

For ye know the grace of our Lord Jesus Christ, that, though he was rich, yet for your sakes he became poor, that ye through his poverty might be rich.   2 CORINTHIANS 8:9

What Child is this, who, laid to rest
On Mary's lap is sleeping?
Whom angels greet with anthems sweet,
While shepherds watch are keeping?

FROM "WHAT CHILD IS THIS?"
BY WILLIAM CHATTERTON DIX

Jesus answered and said unto her, If thou knewest the gift of God, and who it is that saith to thee, Give me to drink; thou wouldest have asked of him, and he would have given thee living water. JOHN 4:10

And ye know that he was manifested to take away our sins; and in him is no sin. 1 JOHN 3:5

But of him are ye in Christ Jesus, who of God is made unto us wisdom, and righteousness, and sanctification, and redemption. 1 CORINTHIANS 1:30

Neither is there salvation in any other: for there is none other name under heaven given among men, whereby we must be saved. ACTS 4:12

O holy night, the stars are brightly shining;
It is the night of the dear Savior's birth!
Long lay the world in sin and error pining,
Till He appeared and the soul felt its worth.
A thrill of hope, the weary soul rejoices,
For yonder breaks a new and glorious morn.

FROM "O HOLY NIGHT,"
BY PLACIDE CLAPPEAU
(TRANSLATED BY JOHN SULLIVAN DWIGHT)

For the wages of sin is death; but the gift of God is eternal life through Jesus Christ our Lord.   ROMANS 6:23

Behold, the angel of the LORD appeared unto him in a dream, saying, Joseph, thou son of David, fear not to take unto thee Mary thy wife: for that which is conceived in her is of the Holy Ghost. And she shall bring forth a son, and thou shalt call his name JESUS: for he shall save his people from their sins.

MATTHEW 1:20–21

This is a faithful saying, and worthy of all acceptation, that Christ Jesus came into the world to save sinners.

1 TIMOTHY 1:15

Who his own self bare our sins in his own body on the tree, that we, being dead to sins, should live unto righteousness: by whose stripes ye were healed.   1 PETER 2:24

He spoke to His beloved Son
With infinite compassion:
"Go hence, my heart's most precious One,
Be to the lost Salvation;
Death, his relentless tyrant, stay,
And bear him from his sins away
With Thee to live forever!"

FROM "DEAR CHRISTIAN PEOPLE ALL, REJOICE,"
BY MARTIN LUTHER (TRANSLATED BY C. G. HAAS)

He that spared not his own Son, but delivered him up for us all,
how shall he not with him also freely give us all things?

ROMANS 8:32

Who hath delivered us from the power of darkness, and hath
translated us into the kingdom of his dear Son: In whom we have
redemption through his blood, even the forgiveness of sins.

COLOSSIANS 1:13–14

Forasmuch as ye know that ye were not redeemed with corruptible things, as silver and gold, from your vain conversation
received by tradition from your fathers; But with the precious
blood of Christ, as of a lamb without blemish and without spot.

1 PETER 1:18–19

For other foundation can no man lay than that is laid, which is
Jesus Christ.

1 CORINTHIANS 3:11

There's a tumult of joy
o'er the wonderful birth,
For the virgin's sweet Boy is
the Lord of the earth.
Ay! The star rains its fire
while the beautiful sing,
For the manger of Bethlehem
cradles a King!

FROM "THERE'S A SONG IN THE AIR,"
BY JOSIAH GILBERT HOLLAND

Thanks be unto God for his unspeakable gift.

2 CORINTHIANS 9:15

❧

And they sung a new song, saying, Thou art worthy to take the book, and to open the seals thereof: for thou wast slain, and hast redeemed us to God by thy blood out of every kindred, and tongue, and people, and nation; And hast made us unto our God kings and priests: and we shall reign on the earth.

REVELATION 5:9–10

❧

The next day John seeth Jesus coming unto him, and saith, Behold the Lamb of God, which taketh away the sin of the world.

JOHN 1:29

❧

This is my beloved Son, in whom I am well pleased.

MATTHEW 3:17

As with joyful steps they sped
To that lowly manger bed
There to bend the knee before
Him Whom heaven and earth adore;
So may we with willing feet
Ever seek Thy mercy seat.

FROM "AS WITH GLADNESS, MEN OF OLD,"
BY WILLIAM CHATTERTON DIX

For by grace are ye saved through faith; and that not of your-
selves: it is the gift of God.   EPHESIANS 2:8

Unto you first God, having raised up his Son Jesus, sent him to
bless you, in turning away every one of you from his iniquities.
                                                    ACTS 3:26

For there is one God, and one mediator between God and men,
the man Christ Jesus; Who gave himself a ransom for all, to be
testified in due time.   1 TIMOTHY 2:5–6

Jesus said unto her, I am the resurrection, and the life: he that
believeth in me, though he were dead, yet shall he live: And
whosoever liveth and believeth in me shall never die.
                                                JOHN 11:25–26

In the little village of Bethlehem,
There lay a Child one day;
And the sky was bright with a holy light
Over the place where Jesus lay.

FROM "THE BIRTHDAY OF A KING,"
BY WILLIAM HAROLD NEIDLINGER

Every good gift and every perfect gift is from above, and cometh down from the Father of lights, with whom is no variableness, neither shadow of turning. Of his own will begat he us with the word of truth.   JAMES 1:17–18

Jesus saith unto him, I am the way, the truth, and the life: no man cometh unto the Father, but by me.   JOHN 14:6

In this was manifested the love of God toward us, because that God sent his only begotten Son into the world, that we might live through him. Herein is love, not that we loved God, but that he loved us, and sent his Son to be the propitiation for our sins.   1 JOHN 4:9–10

But God commendeth his love toward us, in that, while we were yet sinners, Christ died for us.   ROMANS 5:8

From east to west, from shore to shore,
Let every heart awake and sing
The holy Child Whom Mary bore,
The Christ, the everlasting King.

FROM "FROM EAST TO WEST, FROM SHORE TO SHORE,"
BY CAELIUS SEDULIUS (TRANSLATED BY JOHN ELLERTON)

And the Spirit and the bride say, Come. And let him that heareth say, Come. And let him that is athirst come. And whosoever will, let him take the water of life freely.

REVELATION 22:17

And Jesus said unto them. . .he that believeth on me shall never thirst.   JOHN 6:35

Jesus Christ the righteous. . .is the propitiation for our sins: and not for our's only, but also for the sins of the whole world.

1 JOHN 2:1–2

For I am persuaded, that neither death, nor life, nor angels, nor principalities, nor powers, nor things present, nor things to come, Nor height, nor depth, nor any other creature, shall be able to separate us from the love of God, which is in Christ Jesus our Lord.   ROMANS 8:38–39

Rejoice, rejoice this happy morn,
A Savior unto us is born,
The Christ the Lord of Glory.
His lowly birth in Bethlehem
The angels from on high proclaim
And sing redemption's story.
My soul, extol God's great favor,
Bless Him ever for salvation.
Give Him praise and adoration.

FROM "REJOICE, REJOICE, THIS HAPPY MORN,"
BY BIRGITTE CATHRINE JOHANNESSEN BOYE
(TRANSLATED BY CARL DÖVING)

Accepting the Gift

Considering the "unspeakable gift" of salvation through Jesus, what should our response be? Since gifts, by definition, are offered without cost, we have only to receive them. In the case of Christ, we believe, accept our position within God's family, and then seek to live a life of righteousness and purity.

Joy to the world, the Lord is come!
Let earth receive her King;
Let every heart prepare Him room,
And heaven and nature sing,
And heaven and nature sing,
And heaven, and heaven, and nature sing.

FROM "JOY TO THE WORLD,"
BY ISAAC WATTS

But as many as received him, to them gave he power to become the sons of God, even to them that believe on his name.

JOHN 1:12

❧

Behold, I stand at the door, and knock: if any man hear my voice, and open the door, I will come in to him, and will sup with him, and he with me.   REVELATION 3:20

❧

And the keeper of the prison. . .brought them out, and said, Sirs, what must I do to be saved? And they said, Believe on the Lord Jesus Christ, and thou shalt be saved, and thy house.

ACTS 16:27, 30–31

❧

Receive with meekness the engrafted word, which is able to save your souls.   JAMES 1:21

Come, Desire of nations, come,
Fix in us Thy humble home;
Rise, the woman's conquering Seed,
Bruise in us the serpent's head.

Now display Thy saving power,
Ruined nature now restore;
Now in mystic union join
Thine to ours, and ours to Thine.

FROM "HARK! THE HERALD ANGELS SING,"
BY CHARLES WESLEY

For ye have not received the spirit of bondage again to fear; but ye have received the Spirit of adoption, whereby we cry, Abba, Father.   ROMANS 8:15

Having predestinated us unto the adoption of children by Jesus Christ to himself, according to the good pleasure of his will, To the praise of the glory of his grace, wherein he hath made us accepted in the beloved.   EPHESIANS 1:5–6

Know ye not that your bodies are the members of Christ?
                                                    1 CORINTHIANS 6:15

For we are members of his body, of his flesh, and of his bones.
                                                    EPHESIANS 5:30

A silent Teacher, Lord
Thou bidd'st us not refuse
To bear what flesh would have us shun,
To shun what flesh would choose.

Our sinful pride to cure
With that pure love of Thine,
O be Thou born within our heart,
Most Holy Child divine.

FROM "GOD FROM ON HIGH HATH HEARD,"
BY CHARLES COFFIN

30

But as he which hath called you is holy, so be ye holy in all manner of conversation; Because it is written, Be ye holy; for I am holy.   1 PETER 1:15–16

If so be that ye have heard him, and have been taught by him, as the truth is in Jesus: That ye put off concerning the former conversation the old man, which is corrupt according to the deceitful lusts; And be renewed in the spirit of your mind.

EPHESIANS 4:21–23

Wherefore seeing we also are compassed about with so great a cloud of witnesses, let us lay aside every weight, and the sin which doth so easily beset us, and let us run with patience the race that is set before us, Looking unto Jesus the author and finisher of our faith.   HEBREWS 12:1–2

My little children, these things write I unto you, that ye sin not.

1 JOHN 2:1

Adam's likeness, Lord, efface,
Stamp Thine image in its place:
Second Adam from above,
Reinstate us in Thy love.
Let us Thee, though lost, regain,
Thee, the Life, the inner man:
O, to all Thyself impart,
Formed in each believing heart.

FROM "HARK THE HERALD ANGELS SING,"
BY CHARLES WESLEY

Sharing the Gift

Having accepted this wonderful gift, what have we yet to do? An expression of gratitude is always appropriate, especially when the gift is Jesus and the giver is God—who is worthy of all praise. Then there's the final response—sharing the gift with others around us.

Dear Christian people all, rejoice,
Each soul with joy upraising.
Pour forth a song with heart and voice,
With love and gladness singing.
Give thanks to God, our Lord above,
Thanks for His miracles of love!
Dearly He hath redeemed us.

FROM "DEAR CHRISTIAN PEOPLE ALL, REJOICE,"
BY MARTIN LUTHER (TRANSLATED BY C. G. HAAS)

And let them sacrifice the sacrifices of thanksgiving, and declare his works with rejoicing.   PSALM 107:22

Giving thanks unto the Father, which hath made us meet to be partakers of the inheritance of the saints in light: Who hath delivered us from the power of darkness, and hath translated us into the kingdom of his dear Son: In whom we have redemption through his blood, even the forgiveness of sins.

COLOSSIANS 1:12–14

Enter into his gates with thanksgiving, and into his courts with praise: be thankful unto him, and bless his name.

PSALM 100:4

And let the peace of God rule in your hearts. . .and be ye thankful.

COLOSSIANS 3:15

All creation, join in praising
God, the Father, Spirit, Son,
Evermore your voices raising
To the eternal Three in One

FROM "ANGELS FROM THE REALM OF GLORY,"
BY JAMES MONTGOMERY

Sing praises to the LORD, which dwelleth in Zion: declare among the people his doings.   PSALM 9:11

By him therefore let us offer the sacrifice of praise to God continually, that is, the fruit of our lips giving thanks to his name.
                                                    HEBREWS 13:15

Praise the LORD with harp: sing unto him with the psaltery and an instrument of ten strings.   PSALM 33:2

For ye are bought with a price: therefore glorify God in your body, and in your spirit, which are God's.
                                              1 CORINTHIANS 6:20

Go, tell it on the mountain,
Over the hills and everywhere.
Go, tell it on the mountain,
That Jesus Christ is born.

From "Go Tell It on the Mountain,"
By John Wesley Work, Jr.

Go ye therefore, and teach all nations, baptizing them in the name of the Father, and of the Son, and of the Holy Ghost.

MATTHEW 28:19

But ye shall receive power, after that the Holy Ghost is come upon you: and ye shall be witnesses unto me both in Jerusalem, and in all Judaea, and in Samaria, and unto the uttermost part of the earth.

ACTS 1:8

Be ready always to give an answer to every man that asketh you a reason of the hope that is in you with meekness and fear.

1 PETER 3:15

Ye are my witnesses, saith the LORD.

ISAIAH 43:10

Herein is my Father glorified, that ye bear much fruit.

JOHN 15:8

"Glory to God in highest heaven,
Who unto man His Son hath given,"
While angels sing with pious mirth,
A glad new year to all the earth.

FROM "FROM HEAVEN ABOVE TO EARTH I COME,"
BY MARTIN LUTHER (TRANSLATED BY CATHERINE WINKWORTH)